25
ESSENTIALS

TECHNIQUES FOR
GRILLING

25 ESSENTIALS

TECHNIQUES FOR GRILLING

ARDIE A. DAVIS

A.K.A. REMUS POWERS, PH.D.

The Harvard Common Press
Boston, Mussachusetts

The Harvard Common Press
535 Albany Street
Boston, Massachusetts 02118
www.harvardcommonpress.com

Printed in China
Printed on acid-free paper

Library of Congress Cataloging-in-Publication Data
Davis, Ardie A.
  25 essentials : techniques for grilling / Ardie A. Davis.
      p. cm.
  ISBN 978-1-55832-392-6 (case bound, spiral : alk. paper)
  1. Barbecue cookery. I. Title. II. Title: Twenty-five essentials.
  TX840.B3P688 2009
  641.5'784--dc22
                                    2008036448

Special bulk-order discounts are available on this and other Harvard Common Press books. Companies and organizations may purchase books for premiums or resale, or may arrange a custom edition, by contacting the Marketing Director at the address above.

Book design by Elizabeth Van Itallie
Photography by Joyce Oudkerk Pool
Food styling by Jen Straus, with Alexa Hyman and Ashley Quintana
Props by Tabletop Prop

10 9 8 7 6 5 4 3 2 1

FOR DAVID F. EMMOTT, M.D., AND JOHN T. STRICKLAND, M.D.

—friends and barbecue aficionados, as well as gifted, competent, compassionate physicians and surgeons—with my deepest thanks

CONTENTS

SIDES

DESSERT

ACKNOWLEDGMENTS

Thanks to my dad, Art Davis, and my uncle, Chuck Rains, for teaching me how to grill during my growing-up years in Oklahoma City. Rest in peace. Thanks also to my wife, Gretchen, for her endless patience and encouragement.

INTRODUCTION

Grilling—cooking food over hot coals or flames—is done everywhere, worldwide. It is the classic method of cooking food with fire. Practiced for thousands of years, basic grilling delivers rich, uncomplicated flavor.

The goal of each recipe in this book is to show you a particular grilling technique, whether straightforward direct grilling, planking, grilling with a kiss of smoke, grilling right on the coals, grilling indirectly, using skewers or a fish basket or a grill wok, or grilling under a brick. Along the way, you'll also learn how to use a rub, a marinade, a baste, or a glaze; how to manage flare-ups; how to grill and glaze bone-in chicken or pork without burning it; and how to get a steak just the way you like it, whether it's tender and juicy with good grill marks, has a smoky flavor, or is charry-crusted. You'll learn how to use your grill to grill bake a casserole, grill roast a whole chicken, or flash grill a boneless chicken breast on a busy night.

The techniques and recipes in this book are strong on simple flavors, with minimal extra seasonings. I believe that too much seasoning overpowers food's natural flavors. To my mind, the smoky flavor of charcoal and a simple sprinkle of salt and pepper are all that grilled food really needs; however, a finishing sauce, flavored butter, relish, or chutney can add color and variety.

Whether your grill is a basic charcoal kettle or a gourmet stainless-steel gas grill with all the bells and whistles, you can learn how to achieve acclaimed Memphis-style grilled ribs or a planked salmon fillet that will be the envy of your neighbors. It's all in how you manage the fire and add flavor.

So, let's get started!

THE ESSENTIALS OF GRILLING

Grilling is a hot and fast method of cooking food directly over hot coals or flames using gas, wood, charcoal, or charcoal briquets as fuel.

THE MANY FLAVORS OF GRILLING

The fantastic flavors of grilling come from three sources:

- BEFORE GRILLING: Seasonings and marinades offer zest to food before they even get to the fire.

- DURING GRILLING: Many flavors and textures result from the grilling process itself. We're all familiar with the charry "grill marks" on our chicken breasts or burgers that result from the caramelization of the sugars in foods over high heat. In addition, smoky flavors from charcoal or wood chips, sweet and sour seasonings from barbecue sauce, or the woody aromatic taste from a wood plank are all flavors that can be added to food while it is over the flames.

- AFTER GRILLING: Finishing sauces, butters, or chutneys added after the food is removed from the fire can also greatly enhance its flavors.

If you're a charcoal griller, you'll get a smokier flavor from briquets than from hardwood lump charcoal, so that's good to know if you want a smoky flavor on beef, but not on fruit. But we're getting ahead of ourselves now. Don't worry, this book shows you how to do it all, and we'll get there in due time.

BASIC TOOL KIT FOR GRILLERS

I have grilled in brick pits, offset fireboxes, grills made from 55-gallon drums, hibachis, improvised campfire grills, and various other grills. My grill of choice today is a 22½-inch standard charcoal kettle grill. I also have an inexpensive hooded square cooker that I use for backup grilling. Gas grills are great when you're in a hurry. I limit my gas grilling to guest grilling at the homes of friends or relatives. But most of the recipes in this book work for any type of grill you might have.

Once you have your grill of choice, it's time to make sure you have all the essential tools.

- **SHARP KNIVES:** A sharp standard butcher knife is essential for trimming or slicing. Get the best you can afford. Check local restaurant supply stores for bargains on good-quality used knives.

- **CUTTING BOARDS:** My preference is for boards made of hardwood or bamboo. I recommend having at least two cutting boards—one for meat and one for fruits and vegetables. Thoroughly clean the cutting board between uses.

- **LONG-HANDLED FORK:** Keep one handy for when tongs won't do.

- **LONG-HANDLED TONGS:** Stainless-steel spring-loaded tongs work best. They are useful for spreading or moving hot coals in the grill, in addition to handling food on the grill.

- **LONG-HANDLED SPATULA:** A wide, long-handled spatula is especially handy for turning burgers, breads, and sliced vegetables such as eggplant.

- **GRILL THERMOMETER:** Unless you prefer to guess, use a thermometer to monitor cooking temperatures when grilling with the lid on. I use a candy thermometer in a vent hole at the top of the kettle lid, hooked on with baling wire attached to the handle. Higher-end gas grills come with built-in thermometers.

- **MEAT THERMOMETER:** When in doubt, use a reliable thermometer. Check standard charts for doneness temperatures.

- **WELDER'S GLOVES:** I use leather welder's gloves, available in hardware stores or online, to protect my hands from the heat of the cooker. Wear them when dumping hot coals from the charcoal chimney to your bottom grate (also known as the fire grate), when brushing a grill over hot coals, and at all other times when your hands are near fire.

- **CHARCOAL CHIMNEY (FOR CHARCOAL GRILLS):** This is the fire-starting method of choice for most experienced cooks. See "Building the Fire" (opposite) for how to use one of these inexpensive and durable aluminized-steel starters.

- **ELECTRIC CHARCOAL STARTERS:** These are also popular, especially in places where smoke from burning newspaper is objectionable.

- **PERFORATED METAL GRILL TOPPERS:** When you're grilling foods small enough to slip through the grates, use a grill topper. Some are disposable, designed for just one use; others are made to last. Keep them clean.

• **OPTIONAL TOOLS AND GADGETS:** Some cooks regard these optional tools and gadgets as essential: aprons, hats, aluminum foil, grill woks, fish baskets, metal skewers or kebab baskets, clean brick pavers, grill rails, a small bucket of sand for putting out grease fires, a wooden-handled dish mop, and flippers such as the PigTail.

BUILDING THE FIRE

For each recipe, you'll need to start a fire in your grill for either direct grilling (the food in direct contact with the heat) or indirect grilling (the food off to the side of the heat).

Place your charcoal chimney on a nonflammable surface and fill the top of the chimney to the desired level with briquets. Slightly tip the chimney over and stuff one to two sheets of crumpled newspaper in the convex-shaped bottom. Light the paper with a match and place the chimney on your bottom grill grate. In 15 to 20 minutes, your briquets should be glowing, ashed over, and ready to spread over the bottom of the grill.

Use lighter fluid or pretreated briquets as a last resort, and make sure coals are free of lighter residue before grilling.

For a gas grill, simply turn on the gas and set the temperature—usually medium-high. For direct grilling, turn on all the burners. For indirect grilling, leave one or two burners off, depending on how your gas grill is configured. Now you gas grillers are ready to go!

CHARCOAL CHIMNEY TIP: To avoid the danger of dumping hot coals from your chimney, here's a tip from a friend, Dr. Mike Donnelly. Remove the wires at the bottom of the chimney that separate newspaper from briquets. Load and light as usual and place in the bottom of your charcoal grill. When the coals are ready, lift the chimney, and the coals automatically fall into the bottom of the grill.

MANAGING THE FIRE

Learning to manage your fire will allow you to increase what you can do on your grill and produce food grilled the way you want it. If something is grilling too fast and beginning to burn—the most common problem for beginners—there are several adjustments you can make to correct the problem. One is to spread the coals to one side in a charcoal grill or turn a burner off on a gas grill to create a cooler side where you can temporarily place food. But sometimes you want a charry crust on a steak or peppers, so you place the food as close to the flame as possible.

If the recipe doesn't specify closing the lid at any point while cooking, you can assume the lid should remain open.

Here are a few ways to manage the fire.

CHARCOAL GRILL

To decrease the distance between the food and the heat, place more charcoal, several bricks, or a few pieces of wood in the bottom of the charcoal grill so that the glowing coals are closer to the grill rack. To increase the distance between the food and the heat source in a charcoal grill, create an indirect fire, with the coals to one side.

To adjust the temperature on a closed charcoal grill, open the vents wider to raise the temperature and narrow the vents to lower it. Also, using hardwood lump charcoal, especially mesquite, will create a hotter, faster-burning fire than using briquets.

GAS GRILL

Turn the heat to high to get more of a charry crust, and turn a burner off to create a cool zone. To adjust the temperature on a gas grill, simply turn the knobs.

25 ESSENTIALS

TECHNIQUES FOR GRILLING

PLANKED GOAT CHEESE WITH SUN-DRIED-TOMATO AND BASIL PESTO

SERVES 4

Plank grilling is an easy technique used to enhance the flavor of many foods. The technique is to expose the goat cheese briefly to fire, smoke, and wood, just long enough to combine a smoke accent with the aromatic flavor of the plank, and then complement the cheese with the fresh-from-the-garden flavor of pesto. You can buy untreated hardwood planks at hardware, barbecue, home improvement, and grocery stores. Soak the plank in a large plastic garbage bag or in a deep sink, weighted down with a clean brick or canned goods. This method also works with other soft or semisoft cheeses such as cream cheese, Brie, Camembert, or even Gouda (remove the rind from the Gouda first). My wife, Gretchen, and I have served this goat cheese appetizer so many times that it has become one of our signature dishes. There is seldom any left over.

INGREDIENTS

6 ounces dry-packed sun-dried tomatoes

3 cups boiling water

2 large garlic cloves, halved

1 cup fresh basil leaves, or ½ cup basil pesto

½ cup freshly grated Parmesan cheese

⅓ cup fresh flat-leaf parsley leaves

⅓ cup dry red or white wine

Sea salt and freshly ground black pepper to taste

1 cedar plank, soaked in water for at least 4 hours or overnight

1 teaspoon extra-virgin olive oil, for oiling plank

11 ounces fresh goat cheese

¼ cup toasted pine nuts or walnut pieces, for garnish

Whole grain crackers or baguette slices for serving

NOTE: You will have about 1 cup of pesto left over from this recipe. I suggest freezing it for later use on goat cheese or pasta.

METHOD

1. To make the sun-dried-tomato and basil pesto, pour the boiling water over the sun-dried tomatoes in a small bowl and set aside to soften for 15 minutes. Drain, then place the softened sun-dried tomatoes, garlic cloves, basil leaves, Parmesan cheese, parsley, wine, and salt and pepper in a food processor or blender and pulse until blended. Set aside.

2. Fill your charcoal chimney with briquets, set the chimney on the bottom grill grate, and light. For a gas grill, turn to medium. Remove the plank from the water, shake off excess water, and wipe both sides of the plank with a dry paper towel. Rub the olive oil on one side of the plank.

3. When the coals are ready, dump them into the bottom of your grill and spread evenly. Place the plank, oiled side up, directly on the grill grate over the coals or gas burners. Place the cheese in the center of the plank. Close the grill lid and leave the plank and cheese alone for 15 to 20 minutes or until the cheese has bronzed and has a good, smoky aroma.

4. Remove the plank from the grill with welder's gloves. Leave the cheese on the plank and put the plank on a platter, a wooden cutting board, or a dampened hand towel. Top the cheese with $\frac{1}{3}$ cup of sun-dried-tomato and basil pesto and garnish with toasted walnuts or pine nuts. Serve with whole grain crackers or baguette slices.

FIRE-ROASTED PEPPER SALSA

MAKES ABOUT 1 CUP

I love this stuff! Fire-roasted bell peppers make a great appetizer over cream cheese, a delicious side dish, or a complement to grilled steak, chicken, pork, or fish. The trick to getting the peppers really fire roasted is to have the grill grate as close to the heat source as possible. On a charcoal grill, this means putting something like bricks, hardwood, or more charcoal in the bottom of your grill, so when you dump the coals in, they will sit higher, nearer the grill grate. For a gas grill, just crank it up to high. Turbinado sugar is a light brown, unrefined sugar, sometimes found under the brand name Sugar in the Raw; cane syrup is a thick, sweet syrup used in Caribbean and Creole cooking. (I use Steen's cane syrup, but any type will do.) You can find both at specialty markets, some grocery stores, or online.

INGREDIENTS

1 red bell pepper

1 orange bell pepper

1 jalapeño chile (optional)

1 scallion (white part and some of the green), chopped

½ cup turbinado sugar or cane syrup

2 tablespoons cider vinegar

METHOD

1. Place a few bricks, hardwood logs, or about a chimney's worth of charcoal briquets on the bottom of your charcoal grill, leaving some space to set down the chimney starter. Fill the chimney with briquets, set the chimney on the bottom grill grate, and light. When the coals are ready, dump them on top of the bricks, wood, or charcoal. For a gas grill, turn to high.

2. Place the peppers (including the jalapeño, if using) over direct heat. Turn them constantly with long-handled tongs, one after the next, for 3 minutes. Remove the peppers from the coals to a brown paper lunch bag to cool for 10 minutes.

3. When the peppers are cooled, remove them from the bag. Rinse the peppers under cold running water and dry. Remove and discard the pepper stems, seeds, and any blackened skin that is peeling off. Dice peppers, combine with the remaining ingredients in a bowl, stir together, and eat as you see fit.

HICKORY-GRILLED SHRIMP SKEWERS WITH HORSERADISH SAUCE

SERVES 4

Grilling food on skewers—in this case over wood—is a great way to cook and serve appetizers or a main dish quickly. The trick here is to soak the bamboo skewers so they don't burn, thread the shrimp onto the skewers so they touch but are not crowded, then grill until the shrimp are just opaque. Leave the shells on, which protects them from drying out too much. Throwing a handful of hickory chips on the fire gives the shrimp a wonderful smoky aroma. In general, skewers are easy to grill, as long as the pieces of food are roughly equal in size. Although some people don't like to put proteins and vegetables on the same skewer because vegetables get done faster than chicken or beef, there's no worry here because the shrimp cook just as fast as the vegetables. If you like, substitute scallops or squid.

INGREDIENTS

⅔ cup low-fat buttermilk

⅓ cup mayonnaise

¼ cup prepared horseradish

1 teaspoon sea salt

1 teaspoon Dijon-style mustard

¼ teaspoon cayenne pepper, or to taste

8 wooden or bamboo skewers, soaked in water for at least 4 hours

1 pound unpeeled shrimp (51 to 60 count)

24 mini bell peppers (orange, red, and yellow), stemmed and seeded, or 4 medium-size bell peppers (orange, red, and yellow), seeded and cut into 1-inch strips

3 tablespoons extra-virgin olive oil for brushing or misting

1 teaspoon granulated garlic

1 teaspoon freshly ground black pepper

1 teaspoon sea salt

1 cup dry hickory wood chips

METHOD

1. To make the horseradish sauce, combine the buttermilk, mayonnaise, horse-radish, salt, mustard, and cayenne pepper in a bowl and whisk until blended. Cover and refrigerate until the shrimp is served.

2. Thread three mini peppers or pepper strips and two shrimp onto each skewer, alternating the shrimp and peppers (begin and end with a pepper). Brush or spray with the olive oil, then sprinkle with the granulated garlic, pepper, and salt. If you use this technique for jumbo shrimp, use two parallel skewers with each set of shrimp. That way, the jumbos will be easier to turn while grilling.

3. Fill a charcoal chimney with briquets, set the chimney on the bottom grill grate, and light. When the coals are ready, dump them into the bottom of the grill and spread evenly. For a gas grill, turn to medium-high. Throw the hickory chips on the hot coals or place them in a metal container near a burner on a gas grill.

4. When smoke rises from the wood chips, grill the shrimp skewers. Using long-handled tongs, turn the skewers frequently until done, about 4 minutes. The shrimp will look orange/pink and opaque when done. Overdone shrimp will be tough but still delicious. Serve immediately with individual portions of horseradish sauce on the side.

GRILLED CHICKEN WING DRUMS WITH BILLY'S MUMBO RUB AND SAUCE

SERVES 4

Grilling bone-in chicken pieces sprinkled with a rub and brushed with a barbecue sauce is easy if you use the right technique—turn, turn, turn! Otherwise, it's burn, burn, burn! Drums are the meatiest part of the wing and are readily available. If you want to make this recipe with legs and thighs, just follow the same format but grill them 10 to 15 minutes longer. Avid barbecuer Billy Rodgers grew up only a block from where Gretchen and I lived one hot summer in Washington, D.C., but I didn't meet Billy until years later, when he and his family moved to Kansas City. When the talk turned to mumbo sauce, Billy shared one of his recipes with me, which I have tweaked here. Cane syrup is available at specialty markets, some grocery stores, or online— it's a dark, licorice-tasting syrup used in Creole and Caribbean cooking. I use Steen's brand of cane syrup, but any type will do.

INGREDIENTS

2 tablespoons freshly ground black pepper

1 teaspoon sea salt

1 teaspoon granulated garlic

1 tablespoon paprika

6 pounds chicken wing drums

½ cup ketchup

½ cup cane syrup or turbinado sugar

1½ tablespoons distilled white vinegar or sweet or dill pickle juice

2 tablespoons hot sauce (Billy uses Gator Hammock; I like Texas Pete or Louisiana)

NOTE: When serving hands-on saucy foods such as this, I give each guest a damp washcloth.

METHOD

1. To make the mumbo rub, combine the pepper, salt, granulated garlic, and paprika in a bowl. Put the drums in a zipper-top plastic bag, add the rub, seal the bag, and shake until the drums are coated with seasoning. Refrigerate overnight.

2. To make the mumbo sauce, combine the ketchup, cane syrup, vinegar, and hot sauce in a saucepan. Stir while sauce simmers for 5 minutes over medium heat. Set aside to pour over the grilled drums or to serve on the side for dipping.

3. Fill a charcoal chimney with briquets, set the chimney on the bottom grill grate, and light. When the coals are ready, dump them into the bottom of your grill and spread evenly. For a gas grill, turn to medium-high.

4. Grill the drums, turning frequently with long-handled tongs, for 15 to 20 minutes, until done. Brush with the mumbo sauce during the last minutes of grilling or remove the drums to a bowl or platter and cover with the mumbo sauce. Serve immediately.

KISS OF SMOKE RIBEYES, SIRLOIN, STRIPS, OR T-BONES WITH BACON–BLUE CHEESE TOPPING

SERVES 4

If you love your juicy steak with good grill marks and the heady aroma of smoke, then this recipe is for you. The olive oil slather keeps the steak from drying out and sticking to the grill grate, a hot fire ensures good grill marks, a cooler zone helps manage flare-ups, and wood chips scattered on the coals (or placed in a metal container near the heat source on your gas grill) provide the smoke. To make your grilled steak even better, anoint it with blue cheese, bacon, and scallions at the end. For this recipe, it's best to have the steaks at room temperature before cooking them; cold steaks take much longer to cook.

INGREDIENTS

1 cup crumbled blue cheese

¼ cup buttermilk

3 strips hickory-smoked bacon, cooked until crisp and chopped into small pieces

1 scallion (white part and some of the green), chopped

1 teaspoon Worcestershire sauce

4 tablespoons extra-virgin olive oil

2 teaspoons freshly ground black pepper

1 teaspoon sea salt

Four 8-ounce ribeye, sirloin, T-bone, or strip steaks, cut 1 inch thick, at room
   temperature

½ to 1 cup dry pecan wood chips or other hardwood chips

METHOD

1. To make the bacon–blue cheese topping, in a medium-size bowl with a fork stir together the blue cheese, buttermilk, bacon, scallion, and Worcestershire sauce. Set aside to use as a garnish for the steaks.

2. Mix the olive oil, pepper, and salt together in a bowl and slather the mixture with your fingers onto both sides of each steak.

3. Fill a charcoal chimney with briquets, set the chimney on the bottom grill grate, and light. When the coals are ready, dump them into the bottom of the grill, banking them on one side. This will make a cooler space on the grill in order to move steaks away from direct heat if flare-ups get out of control. For a gas grill, turn to medium-high and keep one burner on low or off.

4. To get a hint of smoke, toss ½ cup dry wood chips of your choice on the coals, or place a metal container with 1 cup dry wood chips near a burner on a gas grill. (It might take up to 20 minutes for the wood chips to start smoldering on a gas grill; the closer you can safely put them near a burner, the quicker they smolder.)

5. When you see smoke coming from the wood chips, place the steaks on the grill grate directly over the coals or burners and close the lid for 2 minutes. Open the lid, turn the steaks, and continue grilling and turning every 2 minutes until done to your liking—6 minutes total for rare (125°F on a meat thermometer), 8 minutes for medium-rare (135°F), and 10 minutes for medium (140°F). For a smokier flavor, keep the grill lid closed between turnings. If you get a flare-up during grilling, move the steak to the cooler side of the grill for a minute or so, then move it back over higher heat until done. Serve each steak with the blue cheese topping.

DIRTY STEAK

SERVES 4

Dwight Eisenhower wasn't the first or only cook to grill steaks directly on hot coals, but he was the most famous one to do it. One of many stories about Ike in the Eisenhower Library archives relates that he liked three-inch-thick beef strip steaks—also called New York strip, shell steak, or Kansas City strip—completely covered with salt and pepper, then placed directly on white-hot coals for a rare, charry-crusted steak that can be addictive. Sorry, gas grillers, but no dirty-steak cooking on your grill—you need the coals for this one! I have also grilled thick chuck roasts—similar to Ike's famous three-inch steaks—this way, cooking each side at least 15 minutes directly on the coals, with delicious results. This technique works well for any relatively tender protein of a uniform thickness; branch out and try thick pork chops or even a thick tuna steak.

INGREDIENTS

Four 8-ounce ribeye, sirloin, T-bone, or strip steaks, cut 1 inch thick,
  at room temperature
Fine sea salt and freshly ground black pepper
½ cup (1 stick) unsalted butter (optional), melted
1 lemon (optional) , quartered

METHOD

1. Sprinkle both sides of the steaks liberally with salt and pepper. Set aside.

2. Fill a charcoal chimney with briquets, set the chimney on the bottom grill grate, and light. When the coals are ready, dump them into the bottom of your grill. Cover half of your bottom grate with briquets.

3. When the briquets are white-hot, place each steak directly onto the hot coals using long-handled tongs or a fork. Leave the steaks on the coals for 2 minutes. Turn them over and grill for another 2 to 3 minutes for rare (125°F on a meat thermometer). For medium-rare (135°F) to medium (140°F), leave the steaks on the coals for 1 to 2 minutes longer. Remove the steaks from the coals and brush off the ashes. Spread the melted butter over the top and add a squeeze of lemon before serving, if you desire.

FLORENTINE PORTERHOUSE STEAK ON A TUSCAN HEARTH GRILL

SERVES 4

A cast-iron Tuscan grill is a great way to convert your fireplace hearth into a place to grill. This is especially fun and dandy on harsh winter days. This method and recipe was inspired by watching my friend the late Giancarlo Gianelli, Barbecue Baron of Tuscany, and reading his excellent book of stories and recipes, *The Taste of Memories*. Some Florentine chefs serve the famous Florentine steak with a wedge of lemon, but Giancarlo was strongly in the "no lemon" camp of the debate. Since steaks from Italian Chianina cattle are not available in most American supermarkets, here's a recipe for grilling a porterhouse steak in the Florentine style. You can also grill this on a charcoal or gas grill outside, over high heat. Serve this steak with a traditional Tuscan side dish of warm cannellini beans (page 45).

INGREDIENTS

Four 8-ounce porterhouse steaks, cut 3 inches thick
Extra-virgin olive oil
Sea salt and freshly ground black pepper to taste

METHOD

1. Place the cast-iron Tuscan grill in your fireplace. Fill a charcoal chimney with briquets or hardwood charcoal and light. When the coals are ready, dump them into the bottom of your hearth, about 3 inches under the grate of the Tuscan grill.

2. Brush the steaks with olive oil. Place the steaks on the grill grate. After 7 minutes turn the steaks over and lightly salt the crusty side. After another 7 minutes turn the steaks over and lightly salt that side. Remove the steaks, sprinkle lightly with pepper and more olive oil before serving. The steaks will be crusty on the outside and rare (125°F on a meat thermometer) on the inside. Add more minutes on the grill for your desired level of doneness.

TUSCAN BEANS

SERVES 4

Two 15-ounce cans cannellini beans, drained
½ teaspoon freshly ground black pepper
½ teaspoon fine sea salt
Zest of 1 lemon
1 tablespoon freshly squeezed lemon juice
1 tablespoon extra-virgin olive oil
Rosemary sprigs for garnish

Combine the beans, pepper, salt, lemon zest, lemon juice, and olive oil in a
medium-size saucepan. Heat over medium heat for about 5 minutes, and serve
alongside the steak, with a sprig of rosemary for garnish. These can also be
served cold as a bean salad, if you prefer.

GRILLED FLANK STEAK IN CUMIN-CITRUS MARINADE

SERVES 4

Flank steak, unlike ribeye, is tough and lean. It is less expensive, however, and it takes well to a citrus marinade and medium-high grilling. This great marinade helps turn any tough meat tender and flavorful. The marinating technique also works with boneless pork chops and chicken. I love this served with Stir-Grilled Farmers' Market Vegetables (page 102), which you can grill right along with the steak. Your guests will savor the steak and vegetable combo straight from the grill.

INGREDIENTS

1 cup frozen orange juice concentrate, thawed

1 cup freshly squeezed lemon juice

1 tablespoon granulated garlic

1 tablespoon ground cumin

1 teaspoon freshly ground black pepper

½ teaspoon sea salt

2 pounds flank steak

METHOD

1. To make the marinade, combine the orange and lemon juices, granulated garlic, cumin, pepper, and salt in a bowl and mix well. Put the steak into a gallon-size zipper-top plastic bag; pour the marinade into the bag over the steak. Seal the bag and marinate the steak overnight in the refrigerator until ready to grill.

2. Fill a charcoal chimney with briquets, set the chimney on the bottom grill grate, and light. When the coals are ready, dump them into the bottom of your grill. For a gas grill, turn to medium-high.

3. Grill the steak, turning every 3 minutes, until rare (125°F on a meat thermometer), about 22 minutes. Set the steak aside to rest for 10 minutes, then cut into thin slices across the grain. Serve with stir-grilled vegetables, if you like.

PERFECTLY GRILLED BURGERS

SERVES 4

Sometimes the simplest things are hard to beat, like a perfectly grilled hamburger. But simplicity involves good ingredients and good technique. First, it is essential to select the right beef. Bob Stone, a friend, butcher, and barbecue buddy, says it's best to buy ground meat from a specified cut, like sirloin or chuck, instead of the generic "ground beef." The latter is not necessarily bad, but the quality will vary, since ground beef can come from any part of the animal. When I can afford it, I buy ground sirloin; other times I buy ground chuck. I prefer 80 percent lean burgers for grilling. The fat cooks out and makes for a juicy burger. The second secret to perfect burgers is to use medium- to medium-high heat, so they don't burn.

I have savored charcoal-grilled burgers since my childhood in Oklahoma City, where I lived only a block and a half from the Split-T, a longtime burger joint that cooks its burgers over a charcoal-fired flame. Here's my rendition of the classic.

INGREDIENTS

1 pound ground chuck

Salt and freshly ground black pepper to taste

Mayonnaise

4 whole wheat or sourdough buns

4 slices onion, preferably Texas Sweet or Vidalia

METHOD

1. Fill a charcoal chimney with briquets, set the chimney on the bottom grill grate, and light. When the coals are ready, dump them into the bottom of your grill and spread evenly. For a gas grill, turn to medium.

2. Add salt and pepper to the ground chuck and mix well with your hands. Shape the meat into 4 patties of equal size.

3. Grill the burgers for 7 minutes on each side.

4. Spread mayonnaise on the inside of each bun and top with a grilled burger. Garnish with the onion slices and enjoy.

BARBECUE-GLAZED PORK CHOPS AND STEAKS

SERVES 4

Many backyard cooks are famous for their grilled pork chops. St. Louis pitmasters are famous for their grilled pork steaks. The technique is the same whether grilling chops or steaks—an indirect fire (meaning coals or burners medium-high on one side, low on the other), with barbecue sauce brushed on during the last minutes of grilling for a glazed, not burned, finish. For flavorful and juicy steaks or pork chops, use cuts at least 2 inches thick.

INGREDIENTS

1 cup KC Masterpiece Classic Blend barbecue sauce or other tomato-based barbecue sauce (you could use Maull's, in honor of St. Louis)

1 tablespoon turbinado sugar

1 tablespoon cider vinegar

Four 8-ounce pork chops or steaks, at least 2 inches thick

4 tablespoons extra-virgin olive oil

1 teaspoon sea salt

1 tablespoon freshly ground black pepper

METHOD

1. To make the barbecue glaze, combine the barbecue sauce, sugar, and vinegar together in a bowl. Mix well and set aside.

2. Brush the pork with the olive oil, then season with the salt and pepper.

3. Fill a charcoal chimney with briquets, set the chimney on the bottom grill grate, and light. When the coals are ready, dump them into the grill, and spread them evenly over half of the bottom grate. For a gas grill, turn to medium-high, with one burner on low or off. Place the chops or steaks over direct heat and grill, turning occasionally, for 10 minutes or until almost done. If fat flares up or the meat begins to burn, move it to the cooler part of the grill for a few minutes. Brush the pork chops or steaks with the glaze and grill for another 5 minutes, until the sauce sets into a smooth sheen.

USING GRILLING SAUCES

Homemade and commercially available grilling sauces are meant to add a glazed surface and extra seasoning to grilled foods. Since the glaze is composed mostly of sweeteners such as sugar, corn syrup, honey, or molasses, which tend to burn, apply the sauce during the last few minutes of grilling. This way, you avoid burning the sauce and your meat will look nicely glazed instead of charred.

RENDEZVOUS-STYLE BABY BACK RIBS

SERVES 4

When you want to grill ribs, tender baby backs are your choice. Charlie Vergos, my longtime barbecue buddy and founder of the Rendezvous Restaurant in Memphis, Tennessee, has sold boxcar loads of grilled baby backs to enthusiastic rib eaters since 1948. Now his kids run the Rendezvous while Charlie's legacy lives on. I like the restaurant's slogan: "Not since Adam has a rib been this famous." The Rendezvous sells them "wet," with Charlie's liquid barbecue sauce, or "dry," covered with a special mix of dry seasonings.

When I slow-smoke ribs, I usually remove the membrane from the back of the slab. But when grilling, I leave it on, because the fire tends to shrivel the membrane away from the meat, making its removal unnecessary.

For Rendezvous-style baby back ribs, choose the special Rendezvous seasoning (available at www.hogsfly.com), a mild chili powder, or a dry rub that you like—it's the seasoning that gives ribs their signature flavor. I like to serve these ribs with doctored-up coleslaw: Add chopped sweet red and yellow bell peppers to a bag of prepared coleslaw and mix it in a bowl with your favorite vinaigrette or creamy dressing.

INGREDIENTS

4 full slabs baby back ribs

1 cup Rendezvous or other dry barbecue seasoning, plus more for "dry" ribs

1 cup cider vinegar for "dry" ribs

Bottled barbecue sauce of your choice for "wet" ribs

METHOD

1. Sprinkle both sides of each slab with the seasoning and set aside.

2. Fill a charcoal chimney with briquets, set the chimney on the bottom grill grate, and light. When the coals are ready, dump them into the bottom of the grill and spread evenly. For a gas grill, turn to medium.

3. Grill the whole slabs, turning every 5 minutes, until done, about 45 minutes. The ribs are done when the meat pulls away from the ends of the bones. Just before serving "dry" ribs, sprinkle or spray the cooked ribs with the vinegar and add more dry seasoning. To make "wet" ribs, brush the cooked ribs with barbecue sauce.

TUSCAN SPATCHCOCK CHICKEN GRILLED UNDER BRICKS

SERVES 4

This is another recipe I learned from visiting with Giancarlo Gianelli in his former restaurant near Siena, Italy. "Spatchcock" is a technique in which the chicken is cut down the middle and the backbone removed so that the two attached halves can be grilled flat on the grate. Either remove the backbone of the chicken and flatten it yourself, or have your butcher do it. The technique of placing the foil-covered bricks on the flattened chicken keeps more of its surface on the grill for better caramelization. This method works for any small to medium-size whole bird, from quail to Cornish game hens to a small turkey.

INGREDIENTS

2 tablespoons fresh rosemary leaves, minced

2 tablespoons fresh sage leaves, minced

2 cloves garlic, minced

Juice of 1 lemon

1 tablespoon freshly ground black pepper

1 teaspoon sea salt

One 4-pound roasting chicken, backbone removed and flattened

1 cup extra-virgin olive oil for basting and drizzling

2 clean red-clay paver bricks (available at hardware or home improvement stores), wrapped well in aluminum foil

Fresh lemon wedges for garnish

METHOD

1. Combine the rosemary, sage, garlic, lemon juice, pepper, and salt in a bowl. Lift portions of the chicken skin, making small cuts if necessary, and put pinches of the herb mixture beneath the skin. Refrigerate the chicken for an hour, allowing time for the meat to absorb the flavors.

2. Fill a charcoal chimney with briquets, set the chimney on the bottom grill grate, and light. When the coals are ready, dump them into the bottom of the grill and spread evenly. For a gas grill, turn to medium.

3. When your fire is ready, brush the chicken all over with some of the olive oil and place on the grill. Press the bricks onto the flattened chicken. Every 7 to 10 minutes, remove the bricks (wearing your welder's gloves to avoid burning your hands), turn and baste the chicken with the olive oil (use about ½ cup for basting). Grill for 30 minutes, or until a knife inserted in the meatiest portion of the thigh produces clear juice or a meat thermometer inserted in the thigh registers 160°F. To serve, drizzle with the remaining ½ cup olive oil and accompany with lemon wedges.

GRILL-ROASTED WHOLE CHICKEN WITH CHEESY CORN AND LIMA BAKE

SERVES 4

A grill-roasted whole chicken takes longer to cook than the usual hot and fast grilling of a boneless and skinless breast, but the flavors are fabulous and well worth the effort. The key is grill roasting the chicken indirectly, with coals banked on one side of a charcoal grill or burners turned to medium-high on one side of a gas grill. The chicken sits on the cooler side getting bronzed and plump and juicy. Put the casserole on to grill bake at the same time and before you know it, dinner's ready!

INGREDIENTS

One 3- to 4-pound fryer chicken

3 tablespoons olive oil

1 teaspoon sea salt

1 tablespoon freshly ground black pepper

METHOD

1. Fill a charcoal chimney with briquets, set the chimney on the bottom grill grate, and light. When the coals are ready, dump them into the grill, and spread them evenly over half of the bottom grate. For a gas grill, turn to medium-high, with one burner on low or off.

2. Brush the chicken with the olive oil and season with the salt and pepper.

3. Place the chicken on the indirect (cooler) side of the grill and close the lid. Grill roast for 1½ hours, turning the chicken every 20 to 30 minutes so it browns evenly on all sides. Test for doneness by inserting a knife into the  meatiest portion of the thigh. If clear juice runs from the chicken or a meat thermometer inserted in the thigh registers 160°F (temperature will rise 5 degrees after the chicken is removed from the grill), the chicken is done. During the last 30 to 45 minutes of grill roasting, put the Cheesy Corn and Lima Bake on to grill bake.

CHEESY CORN AND LIMA BAKE

SERVES 4

One 12-ounce package frozen corn, thawed
One 12-ounce package frozen baby lima beans, thawed
8 ounces shredded cheddar cheese
1 cup buttermilk
½ cup (1 stick) butter, melted
2 scallions (white part and some of the green), chopped
1 teaspoon freshly ground black pepper
1 teaspoon sea salt

1. Place all the ingredients in a medium-size bowl and mix well.

2. Transfer the mixture to a seasoned cast-iron skillet (10¼ inches in diameter x 2 inches deep) or a disposable aluminum pan. Place next to the chicken on the indirect side of the grill, close the lid, and grill bake for 30 to 45 minutes or until browned and bubbling. Serve immediately, using the skillet as the serving dish.

NOTE: For a kiss of smoke, sprinkle a handful of apple or pecan chips over the coals or place 1 cup chips in a metal container near a burner on your gas grill.

FLASH-GRILLED CHICKEN BREASTS WITH ORANGE-MAPLE SYRUP SAUCE

SERVES 4

The better quality the chicken, the tastier the result. I like organic, free-range chicken best. Flash grilling means you grill fast over higher heat—easy to do if you halve the chicken breasts lengthwise and then flatten them to a ½-inch thickness before grilling. Steamed or grilled buttered fresh asparagus or broccoli and a crisp white California or New York wine are good complements. Flash grilling works well for any thin, boneless piece of meat—veal, pork, beef, or lamb.

INGREDIENTS

Juice of 2 freshly squeezed oranges

Zest of 1 orange

½ cup pure maple syrup

4 boneless, skinless chicken breast halves, halved lengthwise to make 8 pieces

3 tablespoons extra-virgin olive oil

1 tablespoon fresh thyme leaves

Sea salt and freshly ground black pepper to taste

Fresh orange slices for garnish

METHOD

1. To make the sauce, combine the orange juice, orange zest, and maple syrup in a bowl. Stir until well blended and reserve for later.

2. Brush each breast with the olive oil, followed by a sprinkling of the thyme leaves, salt, and pepper. Put the chicken in a gallon-size zipper-top plastic freezer bag, press the air out, and seal it. Place on a cutting board and roll a rolling pin over the chicken to flatten to about a ½-inch thickness.

3. Fill a charcoal chimney with briquets, set the chimney on the bottom grill grate, and light. When the coals are ready, dump them into the bottom of the grill and spread evenly. For a gas grill, turn to medium-high.

4. Grill the chicken for 2 minutes; turn over and grill for another 2 minutes. Before turning again, brush the up side with ¾ of the orange–maple syrup sauce, flip, and then brush the other side and grill for 2 more minutes. To test for doneness, cut into the thickest part or test with a meat thermometer (160°F for done, as the temperature will rise 5 degrees after the chicken is removed from the grill). If the chicken is pink or underdone, brush with more finishing sauce and grill another minute on each side. When done, remove the chicken from the grill to a cutting board. Cut lengthwise into ½-inch strips and serve immediately with the rest of the sauce. Garnish with fresh orange slices.

CRISPY-SKINNED GRILLED DUCK BREAST WITH CITRUS CHUTNEY

SERVES 4

D uck requires special treatment when grilled or barbecued, and I owe most of what I've learned about the subject to Burt Culver of Culver Duck Farms in Middlebury, Indiana (www.culverduck.com). More than a decade ago, Burt got involved in the barbecue-contest network. His mission was to encourage more barbecuers to add duck to their cooking repertoires. Duck is not yet an official meat category in sanctioned barbecue cooking contests, but thanks in large part to Burt, today's barbecuers and grillers are no strangers to it. Successfully grilling a fatty duck breast requires an indirect fire, grilling fat-side down for most of the time, and moving the duck to the cool side of the grill when the inevitable flare-ups occur. Burt says, "It's like cooking bacon." The chutney, which can cook on the grill along with the duck, adds a tart contrast to the rich duck. Leave the rinds on the fruits, except for the grapefruit.

INGREDIENTS

1 pink or white seedless grapefruit, peeled and chopped

1 seedless orange, chopped

2 seedless tangerines, chopped

1 lemon, seeded and chopped

1 lime, seeded and chopped

1 cup turbinado sugar

$\frac{1}{2}$ cup cider vinegar

1 teaspoon fresh ginger, peeled and grated

1 teaspoon sea salt

1 teaspoon prepared horseradish

$\frac{1}{4}$ teaspoon cayenne pepper

$\frac{1}{2}$ cup golden raisins

$\frac{1}{2}$ cup pecan pieces

$\frac{1}{2}$ cup chopped red bell pepper

Four 4- to 5-ounce bone-in duck breasts, rinsed and patted dry

Fine sea salt and freshly ground black pepper to taste

METHOD

1. To make the chutney, place the citrus fruits, sugar, vinegar, ginger, salt, horse-radish, and cayenne pepper in a blender or food processor. Process the mixture until smooth and pour into a heavy-duty stainless-steel saucepan or a disposable aluminum pan. Add the raisins, pecans, and red bell pepper. Set aside.

2. Fill a charcoal chimney with briquets, set the chimney on the bottom grill grate, and light. When the coals are ready, dump them into the grill, and spread them evenly over half of the bottom grate. For a gas grill, turn to medium-high, with one burner on low or off.

3. Simmer the chutney on the grill over direct heat for 20 minutes and set aside; keep warm.

4. Grill the duck breasts fat side down over direct heat, moving frequently. If the flames become too intense, move the duck to the cooler side of the grill, opposite the fire. Resume grilling when the flames subside. After 20 to 30 minutes, when the fat side is blackened and the fat has cooked out, turn the breasts over and grill the meat side for a minute or two, or until the duck is medium-rare (135°F on a meat thermometer). Remove the duck to a serving platter. Sprinkle each breast lightly with salt and pepper. Serve immediately with the chutney.

GRILLED WHOLE TROUT WITH CORNBREAD STUFFING

SERVES 4

Whole freshwater or ocean fish are delicious when grilled using this simple technique. To avoid the frustration and messiness of fish sticking to the grill, use a grill basket. Oil the basket with olive oil to prevent the fish from sticking to the basket. You'll need two grill baskets for four trout or any similar-sized whole fish that will fit in the grill basket. If you can find young, fresh sardines or mackerel (oily fish that resist sticking), just place them whole on the grill grate, omit the stuffing, and dinner will be ready in no time.

INGREDIENTS

1½ cups dry cornbread crumbs

⅓ cup chopped scallion (white part and some of the green)

⅓ cup fire-roasted red bell peppers, store-bought or homemade (page 22), chopped

One 4-ounce can diced green chiles

2 tablespoons extra-virgin olive oil

1 teaspoon freshly ground black pepper

½ teaspoon sea salt

4 whole trout (1½ to 2 pounds each), cleaned

Olive oil for brushing

METHOD

1. To make the cornbread stuffing, combine the cornbread crumbs, scallion, bell pepper, chiles, olive oil, pepper, and salt together in a medium-size bowl. Mix well and set aside. Rinse the trout under cold running water and pat dry. Brush the grill baskets and the trout—inside and out—with the olive oil. Stuff each trout with one quarter of the stuffing. Place two trout in each prepared grill basket.

2. Fill a charcoal chimney with briquets, set the chimney on the bottom grill grate, and light. When the coals are ready, dump them into the bottom of the grill, and spread evenly. For a gas grill, turn to medium-high.

3. Grill the fish for 4 minutes on the first side, then turn and grill for another 4 minutes. After that, turn the fish frequently until done, about another 2 minutes on each side. The fish is done when it flakes easily when tested with a fork in the thickest part. Remove from the basket and serve immediately.

GRILLED SALMON FILLETS WITH LEMON-DILL BUTTER

SERVES 4

Even if a fish fillet's skin has been removed, you can tell which is the skin side and which is the flesh side—the skin side is always slightly darker. But if you can get a fish fillet with the skin on, the grilling is easier, as the skin helps hold the tender fish together. It's also very important to clean and oil your grill grates before grilling the fish to keep the fillet from sticking or tasting like last night's hamburger. Halibut or any firm-fleshed fish fillet is also delicious grilled using this method.

INGREDIENTS

¼ cup (½ stick) unsalted butter, melted

Zest of ½ lemon

1 tablespoon freshly squeezed lemon juice

2 tablespoons fresh dill, chopped

2 pounds salmon fillets, preferably skin-on

2 tablespoons extra-virgin olive oil

1 teaspoon sea salt

1 teaspoon freshly ground black pepper

METHOD

1. To make the lemon-dill butter, combine the melted butter, lemon zest, lemon juice, and dill in a small bowl, mix well, and set aside. Rub the salmon on both sides with the olive oil and season with the salt and pepper.

2. Fill a charcoal chimney with briquets, set the chimney on the bottom grill grate, and light. When the coals are ready, dump them in the bottom of the grill and spread evenly. For a gas grill, turn to medium-high.

3. Put the salmon skin side down on the grill grate and close the lid. Grill for 5 minutes, turn the fish using a wide fish spatula or two grill spatulas, close the lid, and grill for 5 more minutes. The fish is done when it flakes easily when tested with a fork in the thickest part. Drizzle with lemon-dill butter and serve.

GRILL-SEARED SEA SCALLOPS

SERVES 4 AS AN APPETIZER, 2 AS A MAIN COURSE

Perfectly seared scallops don't have to be a restaurant dish only—you can do these on your grill, too. You'll need a seasoned cast-iron skillet with a griddle topper or a grill pan that you normally use on the stove—the kind that is ridged on one side and flat on the other. You will need to place the skillet or griddle as close to the coals or burners as possible and let it get really hot—hot enough that if you hold your hand about 2 inches from the bottom of the skillet or griddle, you can only leave it there for 3 seconds. One big scallop topped with a squiggle of Mae Ploy Sweet Chili Sauce (a slightly fiery and sweet Asian sauce) makes a great appetizer. Four big scallops with a side dish such as asparagus is a delicious meal. This technique also works for squid, baby octopus, or jumbo shrimp. In addition, it works well for filet mignon—just brush the meat with olive oil, season to taste, and sear for a steakhouse crust.

INGREDIENTS

8 large sea scallops

2 tablespoons extra-virgin olive oil

½ teaspoon fine sea salt

1 teaspoon freshly ground black pepper

½ teaspoon granulated garlic or more to taste

1 cup panko bread crumbs flavored with honey and butter or plain

Mae Ploy Sweet Chili Sauce for serving (optional)

NOTE: You can also put the scallops in a grill basket that's been well coated with olive oil, though you may lose some of the panko coating this way. Grill for 2 minutes on each side.

METHOD

1. Rinse each scallop under cold running water to remove any excess sand. Pat dry and put in a bowl.

2. Stir the olive oil, salt, pepper, granulated garlic, and panko crumbs together in a separate bowl. Coat the scallops evenly with the mixture and set aside.

3. Fill a charcoal chimney with briquets, set the chimney on the bottom grill grate, and light. When the coals are ready, dump them into the bottom of the grill and spread evenly. For a gas grill, turn to medium-high. Place the skillet or griddle on the grill grate.

4. When the skillet or griddle is very hot (see page 86), place the scallops in the hot pan and sear for 2 minutes on each side. Serve immediately, plain or with a squiggle of chili sauce on each scallop if desired.

CEDAR-PLANKED SALMON WITH CHIMICHURRI SAUCE

SERVES 4

If you haven't tried plank grilling and thought it was too complicated, you're in for a treat. Your guests will be wowed by the subtle smoky aroma and cedar wood flavor. You can find nontreated hardwood planks for grilling at hardware, home improvement, grocery, and barbecue stores. Soak the plank in a large plastic garbage bag or in a deep sink, weighted down with a clean brick or canned goods. Use an indirect fire, with the plank on the cooler side. The chimichurri sauce adds a piquant, herbal flavor to the salmon. Feel free to experiment by using this technique with boneless, skinless chicken breasts or other fish fillets such as farm-raised catfish, haddock, halibut, or ocean perch, and/or try other types of hardwood planks—oak, hickory, alder, or maple.

INGREDIENTS

1 cup packed chopped fresh flat-leaf parsley leaves

1 cup plus 2 tablespoons extra-virgin olive oil

⅓ cup cider vinegar

Zest and juice of 1 lemon

2 cloves garlic, minced

¼ teaspoon sea salt, plus a bit more to taste

¼ teaspoon freshly ground black pepper, plus a bit more to taste

1 cedar plank, soaked in water for 4 hours or overnight

One 3-pound salmon fillet

METHOD

1. To make the chimichurri sauce, combine the parsley, 1 cup of the olive oil, vinegar, lemon zest, lemon juice, garlic, salt, and pepper in a food processor or blender and process until smooth. Set aside.

2. Fill a charcoal chimney with briquets, set the chimney on the bottom grill grate, and light. When the coals are ready, dump them into the grill, and spread them evenly across half of the bottom grate. For a gas grill, turn to medium-high with one burner on low or off.

3. Remove the plank from the water, pat dry, and rub the side of the plank the salmon will rest on with one tablespoon of the olive oil. Rub the remainder of the olive oil on both sides of the salmon. Sprinkle the salmon lightly with salt and pepper, and set it on the oiled side of the plank.

4. Place the planked salmon on the cooler side of the grill, close the lid, and cook for 20 minutes. Lift the lid and check the salmon for doneness—if the fish begins to flake when tested with a fork in the thickest part, it's done. If it isn't done, put the lid back on the cooker and grill the salmon for another 5 minutes or until done. Serve the salmon drizzled with the chimichurri sauce.

LIME-AND-CHILE-GRILLED CORN ON THE COB, TWO WAYS

SERVES 4 TO 6

Grilled corn on the cob is a classic favorite complement to all grilled meats, and it's easy to prepare. Try both of these techniques to see which one you like best—shucked corn will have grill marks on the corn kernels and more flavor of the grill; corn grilled in the husk will be more tender and moist. Choose the sweetest variety of corn you can find.

INGREDIENTS

½ cup (1 stick) unsalted butter, melted

½ teaspoon sea salt

1 teaspoon freshly ground black pepper

1 teaspoon mild or hot chili powder

Lime juice to taste

6 ears fresh corn

Fresh lime wedges for garnish

METHOD

1. To make the lime-chile butter, combine the melted butter, salt, pepper, chili powder, and lime juice in a 10 x 13-inch disposable aluminum pan or one large enough to hold all the ears of corn.

2. For shucked corn, remove all leaves and silk and rinse the corn under cold running water. Don't worry if a few silks remain; they will burn off when grilled. For corn grilled in the husk, no preparation is needed.

3. Fill a charcoal chimney with briquets, set the chimney on the bottom grill grate, and light. When the coals are ready, dump them into the grill, and spread them evenly over half of the bottom grate. For a gas grill, turn to medium-high with one burner off.

4. Place the aluminum pan with the lime-chile butter on the cooler side of the grill. Place the corn directly over the heat. Turn constantly with long-handled grill tongs; shucks on the unshucked corn will burn and blacken in places. Shucked corn will be completely cooked in about 10 minutes; unshucked will take about 15 minutes, maybe a bit longer. Test for readiness by checking an ear to see if the kernels are tender. If ready, remove the corn from the grill, shuck if necessary, then place it in the warm lime-chile butter. Turn the corn in the butter to make sure the whole ear is seasoned. Serve on a platter or on individual plates with lime wedges.

HERB-GRILLED POTATOES

SERVES 4

T he easiest way to grill potatoes is with a square- or rectangular-shaped grill basket. In this recipe, fresh herbs warmed by the grill lend a wonderful flavor to the potatoes. You can also herb grill by placing fresh woody herb branches (rosemary, thyme, or lavender) directly on the hot coals in a charcoal grill or in a metal container near a burner on a gas grill. To substitute sweet potatoes or winter squash, par-cook the vegetables first in the microwave until about half done, then finish on the grill. Herb grilling tastes best with vegetables, fish, lamb, or chicken.

INGREDIENTS

4 large baking potatoes, halved lengthwise

8 large fresh rosemary sprigs

¼ cup extra-virgin olive oil or canola oil

Fine sea salt and freshly ground black pepper to taste

NOTE: To add a kiss of smoke to the already grilled potatoes, make an indirect fire by pushing coals to one side in a charcoal grill or turning one burner off on a gas grill. Transfer the grill basket to the cooler side, sprinkle a handful of water-soaked wood chips on the coals or place a metal container containing 1 cup of dry wood chips close to a burner on a gas grill, and close the lid for 15 minutes.

METHOD

1. Fill a charcoal chimney with briquets, set the chimney on the bottom grill grate, and light. When the coals are ready, dump them into the bottom of the grill and spread evenly. For a gas grill, turn to medium.

2. Oil a grill basket and arrange the potatoes in it with a rosemary sprig on top of each half. Lock the basket and spray or brush the potatoes and rosemary with the olive oil, then season with salt and pepper.

3. Grill the potatoes over direct heat, turning frequently, for 20 to 30 minutes, depending upon thickness of potatoes, until a knife inserted in the thickest part of a potato goes in easily. Remove the rosemary and serve.

STIR-GRILLED FARMERS' MARKET VEGETABLES

SERVES 4

Agrill wok is best for preparing this dish. Use vegetables you like in season, cut into small enough pieces that they stir grill quickly. Any combo of vegetables of similar size would work, so you could stir grill all summer long and never have the same dish twice! Try zucchini cut into coins, cherry tomatoes, scallions cut into one-inch pieces, small broccoli or cauliflower florets, small green beans—you get the picture.

INGREDIENTS

1 pound zucchini, sliced into ¼-inch-thick rounds

1 red bell pepper, sliced lengthwise into ¼-inch strips

1 medium-size Vidalia, Texas Sweet, or Walla Walla onion, sliced into ¼-inch rings

2 cups fresh sugar snap peas

¼ cup extra-virgin olive oil

1 tablespoon freshly ground black pepper

1 teaspoon sea salt

METHOD

1. Fill a charcoal chimney with briquets, set the chimney on the bottom grill grate, and light. When the coals are ready, dump them into the bottom of the grill and spread evenly. For a gas grill, turn to medium-high.

2. Combine all the vegetables in a bowl. Add the olive oil, pepper, and salt, and stir to coat. Transfer to a grill wok.

3. Place the grill wok over direct heat. Using wooden paddles or long-handled grill spatulas, stir grill the vegetables until tender-crisp with a little char, 6 to 10 minutes. Serve immediately.

GRILL-ROASTED FOIL-PACK VEGETABLES

SERVES 4

Root vegetables such as carrots, potatoes, parsnips, onions, and garlic take well to foil-pack grilling. Add a burger or a bratwurst for a complete meal. Experiment with combinations of vegetables, meats, or fruit to develop your own favorites. In general, it's best to stick with vegetables that take about the same time to cook, so don't pair cherry tomatoes with winter squash. But cherry tomatoes with rounds of tender zucchini would be great, and they'd only take 20 minutes. For a wonderful foil pack of fruit, slice up a small peach or nectarine and sprinkle on a cup of blueberries; dot with butter, sprinkle with brown sugar and cinnamon, close the packet, and grill for about 20 minutes. To adjust the temperature on a charcoal grill, open the vents wider to increase the temperature and narrow the vents to decrease it. For a gas grill, simply turn the knob to medium-high.

INGREDIENTS

2 large carrots, halved lengthwise

4 small unpeeled red or yellow potatoes, halved

2 small unpeeled sweet potatoes, cut lengthwise into 1-inch-thick strips

1 tablespoon extra-virgin olive oil

1 teaspoon freshly ground black pepper

½ teaspoon sea salt

NOTE: To make this for a crowd, simply make more packets. Smaller packets are easier to handle, and the food grills faster.

METHOD

1. Fill a charcoal chimney with briquets, set the chimney on the bottom grill grate, and light. When the coals are ready, dump them into the bottom of the grill, and spread evenly. For a gas grill, turn to medium-high.

2. Place the vegetables into a medium-size bowl. Add the olive oil, pepper, and salt and toss well. Set aside.

3. Cut two sheets of heavy-duty aluminum foil into 12 x 24-inch pieces. Fold each piece of foil in half. Arrange the vegetables on one piece of the folded foil. Cover the vegetables with the second sheet of foil. Fold and crimp all four sides of the foil to seal the vegetables inside.

4. Place the vegetable packet over direct heat. Close the lid and adjust the grill temperature to 400°F using a thermometer stuck into one of the vent holes in the grill lid. Cook the packet for 1 hour or longer, until the potatoes are tender.

GRILLED SQUASH AND SWEET POTATOES WITH SWEET CINNAMON BUTTER

SERVES 4

When the leaves begin to turn and fall, don't forget your grill! These autumn vegetables need a quick zap in the microwave to par-cook, then you can finish on the grill, complete with a cinnamon-sugar butter. Sweet potatoes and winter squash have more sugars than white potatoes and seem to blacken or dry out faster on the grill, but if you par-cook them first in the microwave, they'll grill perfectly. They're delicious with turkey or pork.

INGREDIENTS

1 small acorn squash, peeled, seeded, and cut into ½-inch-thick rings

1 large sweet potato, cut lengthwise into ½-inch-thick strips

¼ cup (½ stick) unsalted butter, melted

1 teaspoon turbinado or light brown sugar

1 teaspoon ground cinnamon

METHOD

1. Put the squash and potato on a ceramic plate, cover with a paper towel, and microwave for 4 minutes.

2. To make the cinnamon butter, combine the melted butter, sugar, and cinnamon in a medium-size bowl and set aside.

3. Fill a charcoal chimney with briquets, set the chimney on the bottom grill grate, and light. When the coals are ready, dump them into the bottom of the grill and spread evenly. For a gas grill, turn to medium-high.

4. Grill the squash and potato for 2 to 3 minutes on each side, until tender and with good grill marks. Remove to a serving plate, spoon the butter mixture over the squash and potato, and serve.

GRILLED PINEAPPLE AND BANANAS WITH LEMONADE GLAZE

SERVES 4

Use gas or hardwood charcoal when grilling fruits. Fruits absorb too much smoke flavor when grilled over wood or briquets. The trick to grilling fruit is to use fruits that are ripe but not overripe or too soft, then brush them with a glaze to bring out the sweetness. Turbinado is a natural, unrefined sugar; you can find that and cane syrup (a thick, sweet syrup used in Caribbean and Creole cooking; I use Steen's brand) at specialty markets, some grocery stores, or online. When you're grilling fruit and using a sugary glaze, it's most important to start out with a clean, oiled grill grate so the fruit is less likely to stick or taste of previously grilled foods.

INGREDIENTS

8 bamboo skewers, soaked in water for at least 4 hours

4 unpeeled ripe bananas, ends trimmed and cut into 2-inch chunks

1 fresh pineapple, peeled, cored, and cut into 2-inch chunks

½ cup turbinado sugar or ⅓ cup cane syrup

Zest and juice of ½ lemon

METHOD

1. Make a lengthwise slice on the skin of each unpeeled banana chunk to allow easy peeling after the bananas are grilled. Thread the fruit onto the skewers, alternating chunks of banana and pineapple.

2. To make the glaze, put the sugar in a stainless-steel saucepan and cook over medium-high heat until it becomes liquid, about 3 minutes. Stir with a wooden spoon and add the lemon juice and zest. If using cane syrup, simply add the lemon juice with zest and stir, without heating. Set aside.

3. Fill a charcoal chimney with hardwood lump charcoal, set the chimney on the bottom grill grate, and light. When the coals are ready, dump them into the bottom of the grill and spread evenly. For a gas grill, turn to medium high.

4. Brush the skewered fruits with the glaze. Place the skewers over direct heat. Grill for 3 minutes on each side, until the fruit is browned. Remove from the grill and brush again with the glaze. Serve immediately.

MEASUREMENT EQUIVALENTS

LIQUID CONVERSIONS

U.S.	Metric
1 tsp	5 ml
1 tbs	15 ml
2 tbs	30 ml
3 tbs	45 ml
¼ cup	60 ml
⅓ cup	75 ml
⅓ cup + 1 tbs	90 ml
⅓ cup + 2 tbs	100 ml
½ cup	120 ml
⅔ cup	150 ml
¾ cup	180 ml
¾ cup + 2 tbs	200 ml
1 cup	240 ml
1 cup + 2 tbs	275 ml
1¼ cups	300 ml
1⅓ cups	325 ml
1½ cups	350 ml
1⅔ cups	375 ml
1¾ cups	400 ml
1¾ cups + 2 tbs	450 ml
2 cups (1 pint)	475 ml
2½ cups	600 ml
3 cups	720 ml
4 cups (1 quart)	945 ml

(1,000 ml is 1 liter)

WEIGHT CONVERSIONS

U.S./U.K.	Metric
½ oz	14 g
1 oz	28 g
1½ oz	43 g
2 oz	57 g
2½ oz	71 g
3 oz	85 g
3½ oz	100 g
4 oz	113 g
5 oz	142 g
6 oz	170 g
7 oz	200 g
8 oz	227 g
9 oz	255 g
10 oz	284 g
11 oz	312 g
12 oz	340 g
13 oz	368 g
14 oz	400 g
15 oz	425 g
1 lb	454 g

OVEN TEMPERATURE CONVERSIONS

°F	Gas Mark	°C
250	½	120
275	1	140
300	2	150
325	3	165
350	4	180
375	5	190
400	6	200
425	7	220
450	8	230
475	9	240
500	10	260
550	Broil	290

NOTE: All conversions are approximate

RESOURCES

BARBECUE AND GRILL MANUFACTURERS

WEBER-STEPHEN PRODUCTS COMPANY

200 East Daniels Road
Palatine, IL 60067-6266
(800) 446-1071
www.weber.com

Manufacturer of the icon of backyard cooking, the kettle grill, plus a variety of other grills, smokers, and accessories. Search the company's website for the grill that suits you, then buy it locally.

HORIZON SMOKER COMPANY

P.O. Box 737 / 802 North 15th
Perry, OK 73077
(580) 336-2400
www.horizonbbqsmokersstore.com

This maker of top-quality backyard, commercial, and trailer-mounted smokers has one for every occasion. Contact the company's president and owner, Roger Davidson, for information and dealer locations.

ACE OF HEARTS BBQ SPECIALTIES, LLC

1331 Swift
North Kansas City, MO 64116
(816) 471-1333
www.thegood-one.com

Seller of The Good-One grills and smokers, introduced in 1988 in Burns, Kansas, by Ron and Larry Goodwin. The Good-One line of products caught on quickly and has a reputation for quality and dependability. Useful videos and dealer information are available at the company's website.

BBQ PITS BY KLOSE

2216 West 34th Street
Houston, TX 77018-6005
(800) 487-7487
www.bbqpits.com

If your dream is to own a custom-made pit built to your own specifications, David Klose is the man to contact. He's a genius at building creative, functional, top-quality, award-winning barbecue pits. David is also the man to see for standard-design grills and smokers. Check his inventory at the company's website.

CHAR-BROIL
P.O. Box 1240
Columbus, GA 31902-0140
(866) 239-6777
www.charbroil.com

*A leading manufacturer of quality, afford-
able grills, barbecue pits, and grilling
accessories since 1948, Char-Broil offers its
products both in local retail stores and
through its website.*

BARBECUE SEASONINGS
Search for local spice companies first, or
ask grilling friends where they purchase
their seasonings. Here are a few of my
favorite vendors.

VANNS SPICES LTD.
1716 Whitehead Road, Suite A
Baltimore, MD 21207
(800) 583-1693
www.vannsspices.com

*Popular with barbecuers and chefs for its
additive-free quality spices and seasonings,
Vanns offers a wide array of herbs, spices,
and seasoning blends, including a line of
organic spices and custom spice blends.*

ZACH'S SPICE COMPANY
1001 Georgia Avenue
Deer Park, TX 77536
(800) 460-0521
www.zachspice.com

*You'll find only the freshest products at this
reliable source, which specializes in spices
and seasonings used in smoking, grilling,
sausage making, and barbecue sauces.*

WOOD PRODUCTS
When buying wood for grilling, search for
local sources first, including orchards that
may sell or give away pruned branches
from fruit, pecan, or hickory trees. Also
ask friends who grill where they buy their
wood. Here are a few other sources I like.

CHIGGER CREEK PRODUCTS
4200 Highway D
Syracuse, MO 65354
(660) 298-3188
www.chiggercreekproducts.net

*This company sells a wide variety of woods
as chips, chunks, or logs.*

BBQR'S DELIGHT
1609 Celia Road
Pine Bluff, AR 71601
(877) 275-9591
www.bbqrsdelight.com

This company sells wood pellets for barbecuing, for the fastest and easiest way to give your food that great smoke flavor whether you're cooking on a charcoal grill, gas grill, or electric outdoor cooker. You'll find all the most popular woods that barbecuers like to use.

NATURE'S OWN CHUNK CHARWOOD
A.J. Martin, Inc.
51 Graystone Street
Warwick, RI 02886
(800) 443-6450
www.char-wood.com

Nature's Own offers charcoal, wood chips, and wood logs for every barbecuing need.

INDEX

ABOUT THE AUTHOR

Frank Boyer

ARDIE A. DAVIS is an award-winning barbecue expert and the founder of Greasehouse University—the fabled institution behind the coveted degree of Ph.B., or doctor of barbecue philosophy. (The rigorous "degree program" is now overseen by the Kansas City Barbecue Society.) Sporting a bowtie and a bowler hat, Ardie judges on the barbecue circuit under the moniker Remus Powers, Ph.B. He was named a Kansas City Barbecue Legend by *The Kansas City Star* in 2003; he also writes a monthly column in the *National Barbecue News* and *The Kansas City Bullsheet*. Ardie lives with his wife, Gretchen, in the Kansas City area.